# AMAZING STORIES

# WOMEN
# EXPLORERS

# WOMEN EXPLORERS

## One Hundred Years of Courage and Audacity

HISTORY/BIOGRAPHY

by Helen Y. Rolfe

PUBLISHED BY ALTITUDE PUBLISHING CANADA LTD.
1500 Railway Avenue, Canmore, Alberta T1W 1P6
www.altitudepublishing.com
1-800-957-6888

Extreme care has been taken to ensure that all information presented in
this book is accurate and up to date. Neither the author nor the
publisher can be held responsible for any errors.

| | |
|---|---|
| Publisher | Stephen Hutchings |
| Associate Publisher | Kara Turner |
| Editor | Nancy Mackenzie |

We acknowledge the financial support of the Government
of Canada through the Book Publishing Industry Development
Program (BPIDP) for our publishing activities.

**Altitude GreenTree Program** 🌲
Altitude Publishing will plant twice as many trees as were used
in the manufacturing of this product.

**National Library of Canada Cataloguing in Publication Data**

Rolfe, Helen Y.
Women explorers / Helen Y. Rolfe

(Amazing stories)
Includes bibliographical references.
ISBN 1-55153-873-3

1. Women mountaineers--Biography. 2. Women explorers--Biography. I.
Title. II. Series: Amazing stories (Canmore, Alta.)
GV199.9.R64 2003    769.52'2'0922    C2003-911123-7

An application for the trademark for Amazing Stories™
has been made and the registered trademark is pending.

Printed and bound in Canada by Friesens
2 4 6 8 9 7 5 3 1

Cover: Sharon Wood on the summit of Mount Everest
(Photograph by Dwayne Congdon)

*For Jaiden and her Nana*

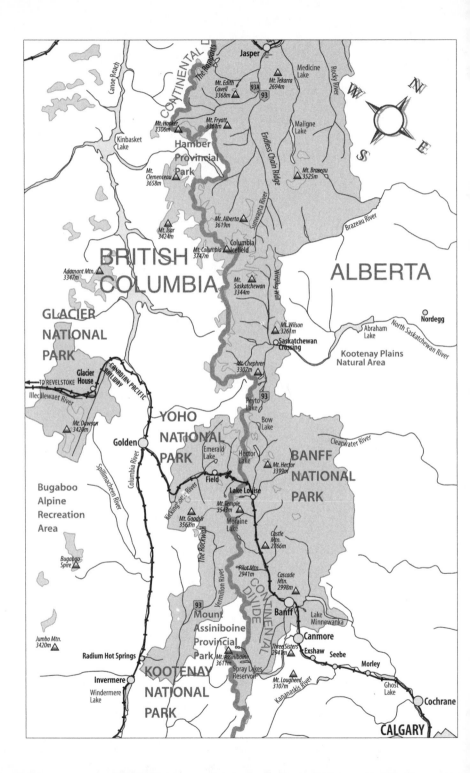

# Contents

# Prologue

*Her pack was anything but comfortable. Thirty kilograms was a heavy load! Her muscles ached, and both feet were sore with blisters. She was exhausted and her energy reserves were running low. She began to doubt her ability to finish the trip.*

*The year was 1999. Leanne Allison was somewhere on the outskirts of Jasper, Alberta, heading 450 kilometres north to Kinuseo Falls, British Columbia — on skis. It was only day three of a month-long journey in untracked snow and deep wilderness. Spring was in the air but the task of breaking trail, melting snow for drinking water, and always trying to stay warm made it feel every bit like winter. The thick forest, avalanche-prone slopes, and high mountain passes that stretched out before her added to the demands and danger of the trip.*

*Leanne adjusted her pack slightly and skied on through the soft, thick snow until she reached a steep canyon. She stared up at the labyrinth of frozen waterfalls that hung like curtains from the huge rock walls.*

*She would have to slowly, carefully, meander up the canyon to reach higher ground. Below was a torrent of freezing cold water, while above hung huge mushrooms of snow perched on icy shelves. The only way through the canyon was along a narrow ledge of ice that stuck out from the canyon wall. Skis off and belly down, she inched her way forward, seemingly suspended in mid-air.*

*The call of the wild that led Leanne here in the first place was silenced by the drum of her beating heart.*

# Chapter 1
# Linen and Lace

A certain kind of person is drawn to the Rocky Mountains. The towering summits and deep valleys dotted with hidden trails beckon both the dreamer and the explorer. The majestic peaks are a beacon of refuge for the body, mind, and spirit, and offer countless adventures. The lure of this attraction is as old as the hills themselves, and it is a place to call home for those who are born with wanderlust. From the early days of mountain exploration right up to the present, adventurous women have felt the pull of these mountains. These women's deeds have earned them a respectable standing in the

history of alpine adventurers.

For Sharon Wood, the Rockies were a starting point. They were a training ground for climbing adventures that would take her around the world, and eventually to the top of Mount Everest. In 1986, she left the Canadian peaks to face the harsh elements and icy slopes of the world's highest mountain. In doing so, she became the first North American woman to reach Everest's summit.

Long before Sharon set foot in the Canadian Rockies, the mountains were deemed an obstacle. The giant peaks formed a seemingly impenetrable wall that separated Canada from east to west. The solution was to build a railway right through the mountains, linking the nation from one coast to the other. In the 1880s, the Canadian Pacific Railway was born, and a gateway to mountain adventure was opened.

The glory days of mountaineering in Canada began in 1886, shortly after the last spike of the railway was driven into the ground. By the early 1900s, women were part of the scene, in quest of their own wilderness adventures. Some were mountaineers; others explored endless backcountry trails on horseback. A few were writers and painters who captured the spirit of the mountains in their work. All of them broke the mould of high society. In an era when women were called ladies, long dresses and bodices were all the fashion, and young girls studied etiquette and needlepoint, adventures in the mountains did not do much for a woman's reputation.

The attraction to the Rockies was strong and the new railway made the mountains easy to reach. At first, well-to-do ladies were content to watch the lofty peaks from the comfort of their rail cars. Slowly, the mountains worked their magic. Hanging glaciers, snow-capped peaks, and skies pink from the setting sun drew even the finest of ladies out into the mountains. Parasols were traded for ice axes, and skirts for knickers. This was a bold statement indeed, as a woman dressed like a boy in these early days was cause for great embarrassment. Wearing pants was an entirely new concept! As one lady climber put it: "I kept unconsciously holding a piece of cloth in my hand when we were walking on the level — I suppose being a girl for so long I had got accustomed to holding up my dress!" Values were certainly changing. The Victorian Age was coming to an end. The ladies were about to make their names known in the mountains, and neither fashion nor expectations of the day were going to stop them.

Gertrude Benham was the first female mountaineer to visit the Canadian Rockies. When she arrived in 1904, wranglers who packed gear to the base of big climbs were not used to a woman's company in the backcountry. As she strode along the trail to the foot of Mount Assiniboine, a half mile would not pass without one of the men checking to see if she was okay. They found it difficult to believe that Gertrude was as fit as a man, and every bit as serious about mountain climbing.

Two years later, Elizabeth Parker became the driving force behind the first, and what continues to be the only, national mountaineering club in Canada. At the time, the American Alpine Club wished to add a Canadian section. Elizabeth Parker insisted on starting a club that Canada could call her own. She was certain there were at least half a dozen people across the country "made of the stuff needed to climb." More than 300 members signed up in the first year, and one quarter of them were women.

While climbers ascended mountain peaks, another woman explored the Rockies in a different manner: on horseback. Caroline Hinman was one of the first females to run adventure trips in the Rocky Mountains. Her trips included everything from trail riding, to camping, fishing, and hunting. A trip with Caroline was more than a brush with wilderness — the briefest adventure was a 30-day trip. *Off the Beaten Path,* her company name, aptly described the style of travel. Rugged and remote suited Caroline just fine.

## Linen and Lace

In 1926, a young Georgia Engelhard fell in love with the Rocky Mountains. Born into wealth and status in New York City, she would later trade the high life for mountain peaks. Mountaineering became such a passion that she would skip an evening's social events to sleep well and wake early for the next day's climb. Georgia had been scared of heights as a girl, but she left that fear behind when she entered her own special world in the Rocky Mountains.

Like her fore-sisters, Leanne Allison loves to explore wild places. Today, a matter larger than personal accomplishment fuels her adventures. She pursues the preservation of those wild places and advocates for the animals that live there. Leanne has traversed mountain ranges, crossed ice-cold rivers, weathered storms from inside a tent, and eaten dehydrated food for months in a row, all in the name of the grizzly bear, wolf, and caribou. She is the continuing thread of women from the past 100 years, of female explorers who dare to dream.

# Chapter 2
# Shaking Hands With Sagarmatha
## Sharon Wood (1957–)

n May 20, 1986 at 9 P.M., Canadian climber Sharon Wood was a long way from home. In fact, she was as far away as possible. She was standing on the summit of Mount Everest, the highest point on Earth. After spending six weeks climbing to the peak, there was no more up to go. She had reached the top of the world. This was an important moment in mountaineering history. Sharon was the first North American woman, and the sixth woman ever, to set foot on the summit of this enormous mountain.

At the time, the excitement for Sharon and her

climbing partner, Dwayne Congdon, was short-lived. They had other things on their mind. Like how to get down. It was late, the sun was setting, and soon darkness would prevail. They still had to climb down almost half a kilometre to the safety and warmth of their tent. Once the sun was hidden, the temperature would plummet to –30° Celsius within minutes and the wind would begin to howl. Neither climber had eaten much for 12 hours. They had been on the move since first light. They were weak with hunger, thirst, and fatigue. Steep rock and ice sections had yet to be climbed down. Their epic day was far from over.

Most of the highest peaks on Earth are found in the Himalayas of Asia. Of them all, Everest is the giant. It is 8850 metres tall, in other words almost nine kilometers above sea level. From the base of the climbing route, the summit of Everest rises 3668 metres straight up. Laid out flat, this is a distance that an Olympic runner would cover in less than 10 minutes. For Sharon and the expedition team she was with, it took 45 days.

Not everyone has the ability or desire to climb the world's tallest mountains. Many mountaineers consider such high altitude climbing too risky to even try. The world's highest peaks are dangerous and difficult. The sad truth is that more than a few climbers have attempted the giants, and have not made it down alive.

Yet there is an undeniable attraction for a small number of people to climb the highest mountains in the world. With Everest as her goal, Sharon was one of them.

Looking back to her days as a child, Sharon had what it took to reach the summit of Everest all along. She hated to sit still and was driven by high adventure. Individual sports were more her style. When her father took her hiking for the first time, at the age of nine, she took off like a rocket. A door had been flung wide open.

Through that door, Sky Pilot, a mountain on the coast of British Columbia, became visible. Climbing this peak would forever change Sharon's focus in life — and climb it she did — at 12 years of age. Her father had arranged for the two of them to join a guided party up the difficult peak. Little did they know then that Sky Pilot would eventually lead to Sky Head, the English translation of the Nepalese word, *Sagarmatha*, for Mount Everest.

By the age of 16, Sharon was determined to pursue a life in the mountains and she set off on her quest. She left her home in Burnaby, British Columbia, and headed for the Canadian Rockies, the heart of mountaineering in Canada. Here, her passion for climbing flourished. The mountains had become her new home and fellow climbers felt like family. Above all, living in the mountains allowed her to remain true to herself — she *needed* to climb. Climbing challenged her body and her mind, it exposed strengths she never knew she had, and most of all, it fuelled her dreams. The more mountains she climbed and the more limits she pushed, the bigger her dreams became. Eventually, these dreams would grow to include *the giant*.

With dreams and hopes come work. A person has to earn a living. Not one to hinder her dreams, Sharon found a job that kept her climbing. She became a certified mountain guide. The job allowed her to guide six months of the year and spend the rest of the time climbing on expeditions in Canada and other countries. This was her ticket to getting experience on the world's highest mountains — a prerequisite for those with Everest in their sights.

At last, after 10 years of climbing big peaks, Sharon's dreams, passions, and hard work paid off. She was asked to join the Canadian Everest Light Expedition team. Of the 11 climbers chosen for the team, she was the only woman. The goal of the expedition was a tough one. They would attempt the peak from the Tibetan side, via the difficult West Ridge, and they would not hire the usual porters to help carry their heavy loads. The result: sheer determination and a strong team effort.

There is a short time period for climbing in the

Himalayas when the days are long and the weather is good. With winter over in March, limited daylight hours in April, and the monsoon season beginning in early June, May is one of the best months to climb Everest. But even then it is no spring picnic. Weather conditions can still turn deadly with the snap of a finger. In an instant, wind speed can more than triple from 30 to 100 kilometres per hour. That is strong enough to blow a climber off her feet no matter how heavy her backpack. Add the constant threat of avalanches, raging blizzards, and sub-zero temperatures, and you have Everest at its best.

Still, the climbers come.

Base Camp, action central, is the starting point for every expedition on Everest. It sits at 5182 metres above sea level, slightly more than three and a half vertical kilometres below the towering summit. Half a dozen teams call this home each spring while they attempt to climb the mountain.

At Base Camp, Jane Fearing, the cook for the Everest Light team, did everything she could to keep the climbers fit and strong by ensuring a constant supply of delicious food. The smell of fresh baked bread that wafted from the cook tent went a long way to help the climbers remain motivated and focused on their goal. During an expedition, climbers continually return to

Base Camp as they gradually make their way up the peak. They do this for several reasons: to re-supply with gear and food, to wait out storms, and to slowly get used to climbing at higher elevations. It takes a long time, weeks in fact, to climb up and down, and up and down the mountainside. By returning frequently to Base Camp, climbers are able to regain their strength and energy in the best place possible — at a lower elevation. Jane's bread was always ready.

As they climb, teams leapfrog their way up the mountain in smaller groups. Each group is responsible for building another camp farther up the mountain while the others recover at the base. It was in this style that the Everest Light team established six camps up the planned route. Camp Six was to be the high point from which a one-day attempt for the summit would take place — if everything went as planned.

At higher elevations, the air pressure is lower. Lower air pressure means less oxygen in the air. For the climber, less oxygen makes breathing a struggle and blood flow slower. Clear thinking becomes nearly impossible. Fingers and toes freeze quickly and the brain limits muscle activity. Even a world-class mountaineer is reduced to feeling clumsy.

The Everest Light team carried bottled oxygen to make breathing easier. On Everest, even that posed problems. First, the climbers had to ferry the extra oxygen up to the high point on the mountain where it was needed. Second, the bottles were heavy. On the final days, close to the summit, the weight of the bottles increased pack loads from 15 to 30 kilograms. The slow flow rate of oxygen from the bottles barely made up for the energy expended carrying the extra weight.

Nothing is easy at high altitudes. Even the basics — eating, drinking, sleeping — are no longer simple tasks. It took Sharon and her partner at least two hours each morning to melt snow for the day's water supply. Operating the stoves was a challenge. High winds made the portable stoves impossible to work outdoors so they had to be lit inside the tent. Open flame, nylon material, and close quarters — a dangerous mix! While one person tended to the stove and made breakfast, the other remained huddled in a down sleeping bag, careful not to move for fear of setting the tent on fire.

With an average temperature of –20º Celsius (and that was inside the tent) meals were not a relaxed event. A dish of canned bacon, fried sausage, or instant oatmeal was gulped down before frost could form on the surface. Warm tea was sucked back as a last-ditch effort to stay hydrated for the entire day. Sharon carried only one litre of water to drink while she was climbing. She had to wait until nighttime to consume the remaining four or five litres of her liquid rations. She felt thirsty all the time.

At high altitudes, getting undressed was tricky. A glove could not be taken off without the risk of instant frostbite. Exposed skin was absolutely forbidden. Team members had been outfitted with custom-fit suits, each layer tailored perfectly to their body. Each climber's face was covered completely with a neoprene mask, and topped with a hat and hood. There were no extras. Each layer was made of the lightest, most supple material designed for comfort and ease of motion. There was polypropylene, heavy fleece, a wind suit, and the ultimate — a down outer layer. The suits were so finely made they felt like they were lined with silk, a small comfort soon forgotten in the harsh elements of the mountain. The team climbed and slept dressed in layer upon layer.

The days passed. Metre after metre of rope was fixed up the mountainside. The team moved slowly from one camp to the next. Weather conditions were changing for the worse and the chances of succeeding on the climb were shrinking. The health of the team members began to deteriorate. The demands of climbing at such high altitudes withered stamina and one by one the climbers had to retreat to Base Camp. By the time Camp Five was ready, only half of the team was in reasonably good health. With such a small number of fit climbers, it would be tough to supply the next camp with gear, let alone reach the summit. They pushed on.

As a team nears the top, members are paired up for the final leg of the climb. Since it is rare for an entire expedition team to reach the summit, choosing the pair that will go first is not easy. The team leader must consider factors such as the health of the climbers, weather, and safety, and then call the shots. In this case, leader Jim Elzinga had another timely fact to face. His team had a chance to get the first North American woman on the peak of Mount Everest. An American team was also climbing on the mountain and they were hoping to get their female climber to the summit first. Up to this point, Sharon admits she never thought about the "woman thing." Sharon was a part of the Everest Light Expedition because she had earned her place. She was equal to her fellow teammates in her skill level and ability. She deserved to be there, not because she was a woman, but because she was a mountaineer. Still, she had a decision to make. To her it was a given that Dwayne and Barry Blanchard would be the first two of the Everest Light team to make a bid for the summit. If all went well, and the weather was good, she would follow. Leader Jim Elzinga, however, made another decision, to strive for a Canadian first. Go for it, Sharon! he urged. This was Sharon's chance to make history.

Sharon had a lot to think about. It meant asking Barry to give up his chance to reach the summit. Barry had worked hard to be there, and he deserved the opportunity to reach the summit as much as anyone. Letting Sharon attempt the summit first meant he might risk losing his chance altogether.

Time was running out. The weather continued to get worse. The healthy bodies of the mountaineers were in a rapid state of decline. For their own safety, Jim could pull them off the mountain at a moment's notice and no one would reach the peak of Everest.

Four of the team — Sharon, Dwayne, Barry, and Kevin Doyle — were strong enough to continue. From the next camp, the summit would be only one day away. Yet Barry selflessly gave up his spot to Sharon. Instead of reaching the summit themselves, he and Kevin would use all their strength and will power to help Sharon and Dwayne get to the top. This was truly a show of team commitment.

As she continued to climb, Sharon veered between feeling positive about reaching the summit and wanting to go home. She was overwhelmed by the huge responsibility that now lay upon her. Fear crept in.

When hurricane-force winds buffeted the climbers and a rock avalanche swept past, barely missing her, Sharon felt like the odds were against them. She had to dig deep for the strength to move on. She found her inspiration in thoughts of her original desire to climb Everest. She wanted to have the chance to perform physically and mentally better than ever before, to find out if she had what it took to reach the summit, and to be with people who shared her passion for the mountains. Above all, she remembered that when the Canadian team had ascended Mount Everest four years earlier, she had wanted to be there the next time her country's flag was unfurled on the peak.

The "next time" had arrived. Barry and Kevin spent every last bit of energy helping Sharon and Dwayne establish Camp Six. From here, the climbers parted ways. Barry and Kevin went back down to Base Camp, and Sharon and Dwayne headed for the summit.

She does not recall how cold it was the day she and Dwayne struggled to the top of Mount Everest. She didn't want to know and not once did she so much as glance at a thermometer during her entire time on the mountain. On this day, her one shot at the summit, she had no ability to register such facts anyway. Instead, every bit of concentration was focused on placing one foot in front of the other. Slowly, she and Dwayne moved away from Camp Six. Fear and doubt began to slowly slip away too.

"Ya gotta want it!" echoed in Sharon's ear. She had

heard these words months earlier from her team leader. At that time, the words were enough to motivate Sharon to run up the stairs of the CN Tower in Toronto — three times in a row! This time they would help her up Everest. She felt a surge of adrenalin as she heard Jim's voice crackle over the radio in her pocket: "Ya gotta want it!"

Sharon and Dwayne had less than 10 metres to go. Or so they thought. It was like the two of them were kids again, sitting in the back seat of a car on a long road trip. "We're almost there," a parent would say. "It's just around the corner." How many corners can there be? Each time they thought they were close to the summit, the mountain extended upwards. It took another hour to cover the ground they thought would take minutes.

Sharon continued her struggle against the extreme fatigue she felt. She willed herself up, up, up. Finally, she glanced ahead to Dwayne to check on their progress. There in front of her, only a few steps away, was the summit of Mount Everest. They had made it!

The view from the top of the world is without a doubt endless and the 20 minutes Sharon and Dwayne spent on the summit were hardly enough to take it all in. They hugged, they unrolled the small Canadian flag Sharon carried in her pocket, and they snapped some photographs. Without warning, the wind ripped the flag out of Sharon's hand, a timely reminder that Mother

Nature never rests. Rest was the one thing the two climbers needed most and to earn it, they had to descend.

At this point, the odds were piling up against them. The amount of bottled oxygen they had planned to use for the day was close to running out. They still had to climb down steep rock walls and ice-hard snow slopes on the descent to Camp Six. They were exhausted and it was getting dark. That nagging reminder of climbers who had failed to make it down in the past was ever-present. The mountain seemed even more dangerous than before.

These factors added up to one thing for Sharon: Focus! She arrived at the first steep rock section where she had to set up ropes for their descent. As a climber, she had performed this task thousands of times — hammer in a piton, clip a carabiner, thread the rope. Never before had this task held such serious consequences if she made a mistake. She and Dwayne would have to trust their entire weight on that anchor as they worked their way down the ropes. She did her job, checked and double-checked her work, and committed herself to the ropes. Years of experience paid off. Even in an oxygen-deprived state, she still knew what to do. Down they went.

It was not until slightly farther down the mountainside that her mind really began to play tricks on her.

## Shaking Hands With Sagarmatha

There was a point where, just the day before, Sharon and Dwayne had carefully secured 120 metres of rope over the steepest section of ground, in preparation for their return. When they reached the ropes on their way home, they had to descend, one person at a time. Sharon went first. She reached the bottom of the ropes in half an hour. Or was it longer? She had no idea. Time made no sense anymore. She waited. No sign of Dwayne. She waited some more. Silence. The lack of oxygen was making her mind shut off. The cold took over and lulled her to sleep as she stood attached to the end of the rope. She awoke with a start. Was that Dwayne she heard? She dozed off again. Again, she was awake. Was that the light from his headlamp she could see high above? No. Nothing had changed. Cold, tired, low on oxygen, in the dark, and alone on Mount Everest — it was impossible to focus any longer.

She had to go on. Convinced her partner must simply be moving slowly, she left the ropes and began her search for their tent. An hour or so passed. Fear rushed in. Where was the tent? Sharon searched around in the snow under the dark sky. The beam of her headlamp was the only source of light. By pure luck she caught a flash of something silver in the snow — a used oxygen bottle lying by the tent. For the second time that day, she had reached her goal — first the summit, now the tent.

Six hours had passed since she stood on top of Everest.

At least now she was safe. It would be another hour and a half before Dwayne reached the tent and was safe too. He had had his own nightmare to deal with. Soon after he and Sharon had separated to descend the steep section, he ran out of oxygen. As a result, breathing was nearly impossible. His fingers and toes were turning to ice fast. Every few steps he had to stop and shake some feeling into them. His descent was painfully slow.

At Base Camp, the rest of the team did not know what to think. The last radio contact they had was an hour before Sharon and Dwayne had reached the summit. The evening had come and gone, and as darkness settled, all they could see were two pinpricks of light coming down the mountain. To add to their concern, the lights they could see were growing farther and farther apart from one another, until finally, both disappeared into the night. No one at Base Camp slept.

Only one thing stopped Sharon and Dwayne from drifting off into a sleepy state once they were in the tent: painfully dry mouths. They needed water. Unaware of an earlier propane leak, Sharon lit the stove and BOOM! It exploded in her face. The stove shot out the door in a ball of flames, and flew down the side of the mountain. Any chance of a drink was gone.

With no stove to tend to in the morning, they set off

straight down the mountain. As they organized their gear for the remainder of the descent, Dwayne handed over something he had found at the summit — a radio antenna. He hadn't realized it belonged to their radio or that it had fallen out of Sharon's pocket. Nor had she. No wonder their radio had been silent for so long. They turned it on and announced their victory to a breathless Base Camp. The Canadian Light Expedition team — and the first North American woman — had reached the summit of Mount Everest. They were on their way home.

# Chapter 3
# Embroidered Edges
## Gertrude Benham (1867–1938)

n the summer of 1904, an English climber named Gertrude Benham arrived in the hamlet of Laggan, Alberta. Nestled in the heart of the Canadian Rockies, this small village — now called Lake Louise — had seen many mountaineers before, but never a female one. Gertrude was one of the very first. During a short but triumphant visit, she proved that women too could be serious mountaineers. This was a new concept in the Canadian climbing circle. In the previous 20 years of the country's mountaineering history, men had been the sole adventurers. A woman's touch was reserved for the household,

not the rugged outdoors. No doubt, Gertrude, dressed in woollen knickers, a starched white blouse, and with a neatly tied silk scarf around her neck, turned more than a few heads in her day.

Unlike many others who returned to these mountains year after year to climb, Gertrude spent only one summer in the Canadian Rockies. She reached the summit of more peaks during that single climbing season than some mountaineers have in a lifetime. Her approach was simple: Be prepared. Gertrude arrived armed with experience. She had climbed several mountains in the European Alps, and was fit and strong. Above all, she was determined. Knowing her trip would be short, Gertrude focused on her number one priority — climbing!

As was customary in the early days of mountaineering, Gertrude hired mountain guides to accompany her on her chosen routes. At the time, the Canadian Pacific Railway brought trained guides over from Switzerland to help promote the newly built railway that ran through the heart of the Rockies. Slogans such as "Visit the Rockies! Climb the Peaks!" enticed adventurers to the glaciers and jagged mountaintops. Under the direction of the Canadian Pacific Railway, the responsibility of the guides was to provide a safe and enjoyable outing for passengers as they stepped off the train platform and into the wilderness.

The first stop for Gertrude was Mount Lefroy, the 34th highest peak in the Rockies and one of the giants that overlooks Lake Louise. On a beautiful morning in late June, Gertrude and her guides, brothers Hans and Christian Kaufmann, started along the shore of the lake. Their route involved climbing Victoria Glacier to Abbott's Pass and upwards to the peak of Lefroy. By the time they reached the toe of the glacier, the weather had changed. The reddish glow of the wee hours had dampened to a grey, overcast sky. It began to snow. Convinced the weather would improve, the party pressed on to Abbot's Pass.

Abbot's Pass was named after Philip Stanley Abbot, a notable mountaineer in the late 1800s who died when he fell from Mount Lefroy. His death was the first in Canadian mountaineering and it was the catalyst for the Canadian Pacific Railway's decision to hire trained guides who could ensure the safe passage of visitors in the mountains. In 1922, a hut was built at the pass in memory of Abbot. Since then, many mountaineers have weathered out storms in the Abbot Hut.

It was at this pass that Gertrude voiced her concern about the weather. It was 18 years before the hut was built, and with nowhere to shelter she suggested they head back down to the comforts of the valley. Her guides seemed to agree. However, as Gertrude would later tell in her writings, instead of turning down the pass, Christian led the way up the snow slope of Lefroy. The Kaufmann brothers were certain they could make it to the top despite the bad weather. Gertrude had no choice but to follow.

Buried in a sea of mist and cloud, Lefroy's peak was hidden from view as they climbed. Each time Gertrude thought they were near the top, a glimpse of rock above forced her to keep going. It was a difficult climb. The weather worsened and the bitterly cold wind and piercing snowfall stung her face. After several hours, icicles had formed and hung from her hair. Although Gertrude must have had second thoughts about her guides' decision to continue up the mountainside, she remained close behind them.

There is an area on glaciated mountains called a *bergschrund.* This is a gaping crevasse that separates the head of the glacier from the rock face of the mountainside. After the winter, these crevasses are filled with snow, making them safe to cross — sometimes. As Gertrude's party reached the bergschrund on Mount Lefroy, a loud crack bellowed through the air. In the same instant, Christian disappeared into the chasm. The bridge of snow that had spanned the bergschrund collapsed from under him as he crossed. Luckily, the team was roped together, and the climbers on the surface could hold his fall. Within minutes, they pulled Christian out of the frozen crevasse. Without batting an eye, he continued to lead the way up the mountain.

Much to Gertrude's delight, they made it to the summit. The view, however, offered nothing spectacular. Everything was cloud-covered. There was no hint of the mountain skyline that surrounded them, or of the beautiful lake below where their climb had begun. It was cold and snowing and their time on the summit was brief. They quickly shook hands and started their descent.

Once the team was beneath the cloud layer and into better weather, they stopped for "refreshments." Gertrude had not eaten a morsel of food for seven hours. She had been on the go since four o'clock that morning. Not that any of this mattered since Gertrude had "bagged" her first peak in the Rockies. It was worth every bit of discomfort.

During her first few weeks in Canada, Gertrude climbed more than 16,500 metres — the same distance as climbing Mount Everest from Base Camp four and a half times. She continued to climb in a frenzy through August and September, setting foot upon all the major summits, including Mounts Victoria, Whyte, and Temple, and Popes Peak.

Claiming a first ascent has always been a large part of the attraction for mountaineers. It guarantees the climber's name in the history books, but more importantly it adds a certain cachet to the experience of the climb. There is something special about being the first person in the world to stand atop a summit.

There remain today a few unclimbed peaks in the Canadian Rockies. They are difficult to access though, located far from any road or trailhead, and they are smaller in stature. Climbers long ago reached the summits of the tallest mountains. When Gertrude visited the Rockies, there were still many unclimbed peaks to be bagged and some of them were the highest in the range. Mount Fay, for one, is a fair size at 3234 metres, and in 1904, it had yet to see a first ascent.

Often a peak is named after the person who first climbs it. This was not the case with Mount Fay. A well-known and influential American climber, Charles Fay, had the honour of this peak bearing his name before he or anyone else had reached the summit. In 1904, he set out to prove himself worthy of the honour. His attempt, however, was unsuccessful.

On the same day, but by a different route, Gertrude and her guide Christian also had plans to climb the mountain, and they beat Fay's party to it. When Fay found out, he was furious. His mountain had been stolen, and by a woman, no less. To top it off, the guide Fay had hired was Christian's brother, Hans. Certain the brothers must have known about each other's plan to summit the mountain, Fay accused them of botching his attempt on purpose. Miffed, he requested that his name to be given to another mountain instead, one that he would be certain to climb first. Much to his disappointment though, someone else — maybe even Gertrude — had already climbed the second peak he chose. In the end, he tried to have the two guides fired by the Canadian Pacific Railway for misconduct.

Unaware of the commotion her climb on Mount Fay had caused, Gertrude continued her quest by climbing Mounts Allen, Bowlen, and Stephen. She racked up her achievements, one after the other.

Later that summer, another first ascent by Gertrude again proved her worth as a mountaineer. She was the first woman to stand on the summit of Mount Assiniboine. To this day, the 3618-metre peak, and seventh highest in the Rockies, is a much sought-after climb by experienced mountaineers.

News of her ascent of Assiniboine made it in to the newspapers, but the stories hardly gave Gertrude Benham the credit she deserved. Even *her* writing barely hinted at the seriousness of the climb. Gertrude's article spoke of a "favourable" day on the mountain, with a view that was "grand and distinct." There was no word of her being the first lady ever to set foot on this most impressive peak. It would be another 30 years before newspaper headlines would champion women's accomplishments in the mountains.

As the months unfolded, two things kept Gertrude busy — her checklist of peaks to climb, and her knitting and embroidery. Hard to believe today, but mastering needlework really paid off. By selling her handiwork, Gertrude topped up an inheritance that allowed her to climb. She also saved money by making her own clothes. At night, when the mountain guides pulled out their pipes for a relaxing time around the campfire, Gertrude set to work with her knitting needles. Much of her time was spent darning and repairing her clothes, which had taken a beating in the thick valley bush on the way to or from a climb.

By fall, Gertrude had shifted her focus to the Selkirk Mountains in eastern British Columbia. The Selkirks at that time were a hotspot for the visiting mountaineer because there were countless unclimbed peaks awaiting first ascents. The peaks were daunting, with huge glaciers, thick forest, and deep snow (12 metres of accumulation was not uncommon in winter).

The mountains formed a barrier that separated British Columbia from the rest of Canada. Until the late

1800s, these mountains had been one of the most inaccessible regions of Canada with no road or rail access. This changed in the 1880s with the advent of the Canadian Pacific Railway. The proposed route cut right through the middle of the Selkirk Mountains. But it was no easy task to build in this environment.

Massive wooden bridges had to be built across the many raging creeks. Engineers had to design ingenuous structures to deal with the steep mountain grades, and at great cost, miles of snow sheds had to be built to protect the tracks from the countless avalanches that thundered down from the slopes above. In the winter, heavy snowfalls made the upkeep of the railway nearly impossible. During the summer dry spells, the wooden bridges stood like matchsticks waiting to burn.

Despite all odds, the railway was completed in 1885, and access to these mountains was facilitated. The CPR even built Glacier House, a hotel at Rogers Pass, the highest point of the route through these mountains. When Glacier House first opened its doors, it was a simple dining car with only enough room for half a dozen overnight guests. The car was set up like a permanent fixture alongside the railway tracks, and over the years, as the reputation of Glacier House grew, it evolved into a grand hotel. A gigantic glacier almost a kilometre long flowed down from the mountainside above. There, at the toe of the Great Glacier — now called the Illecillewaet — many a climber began his or her adventures.

Gertrude stayed at Glacier House and her list of climbs grew: Mounts Sir Donald, Sifton, Dawson, Deville, Bonny, Rogers, and the Swiss Peaks. She scaled them all. In honour of her short visit to Rogers Pass and her astounding mountaineering feats in Canada, the Truda (from Gertrude) Peaks in the Selkirks were named after her.

Once winter was on its way and the climbing season in Canada was over, Gertrude left for home in England — the long way around. She stopped in New Zealand, Japan, Australia, India, Egypt, Corsica, and finally, England. Her travels did not stop there. For the next 30 years she travelled around the world eight times. She continued to fund her trips by selling or trading her fine embroidery work. Her expeditions were extraordinary. On one trip, she spent 11 months walking 6000 kilometres across the continent of Africa. On another, she became the first woman to reach the summit of Africa's highest peak, Mount Kilimanjaro.

Gertrude's accomplishments in the mountains were astonishing. Her successes were equal to those of many male climbers of the era. Her remarkable summer of 1904 stands out as a milestone in female mountaineering. Gertrude broke the mould and opened the door for other women adventurers to follow.

After a lifetime of adventure, Gertrude Benham died at the age of 71 on a steamship sailing back to England. A true explorer of the world, she was buried at sea.

# Chapter 4
# Inkbottle Blue
## Elizabeth Parker (1856–1944)

*"The pen is mightier than the sword."*
Edward Bulwer-Lytton, 1803–1873

lizabeth Parker was an explorer of a different sort. Although she was certainly a seeker of adventure, she sought the adventures for others. Elizabeth was determined to draw Canadians to the mountains while she admired the snow-clad peaks from afar. She succeeded a hundred times over, and she did so with a very persuasive tool: the written word. While climbers swung ice axes into the frozen snow of a glacier, Elizabeth wielded her pen. It is arguable that the excitement and passion with which she wrote did more for the sport of

Elizabeth Parker — adventurer and visionary

mountaineering in Canada than did the efforts of the first climbers who ascended the majestic peaks.

Elizabeth was born in Nova Scotia on Canada's East Coast in the mid-1800s. When she was still a toddler, her mother died and, in time, her father remarried. It was her stepmother who opened the door to a world of writing. There were no telephones in those days, and no televisions to provide a distraction. There were, however, plenty of books to read. Reading was an endless source of entertainment, education, and escape. When her stepmother became ill, Elizabeth diligently read aloud at her bedside. Under the ailing woman's guidance, Elizabeth learned the skills of fine writing, and as she grew older, her taste for literature blossomed. Eventually, this led Elizabeth to become the only literary critic in the country to write a daily newspaper column. Starting in 1904, her articles ran every day for nearly 40 years.

After marrying at the age of 18 — the norm in those days — Elizabeth and her husband, Henry John Parker, moved to Winnipeg, Manitoba. A decade later, she visited the Rocky Mountains on a trip that was bittersweet. Bitter because it was Elizabeth's poor health that brought her to Banff in the first place to recuperate, and sweet because the time she spent there triggered a love for the mountains that would last the rest of her life. After all, it was the fresh mountain air and the mineral waters of the natural hot pools that re-energized Elizabeth and she forever appreciated the healing powers of the Canadian Rockies.

Rejuvenated after a year and a half in the mountains, Elizabeth and her three children returned to their family home in Winnipeg. She continued with her job as a writer for the *Manitoba Free Press* newspaper, and began submitting stories about mountain life. The voice in her articles was inviting: "The sight of a falling avalanche is very rare, and a most thrilling spectacle .... For pure delight a glacier is seen best under the enchantment of distance." Her words also could cut like a knife. If she disagreed with an argument someone had made, that person would get a cutting response. And that is how Arthur Oliver Wheeler came to know of Elizabeth Parker — by running into the sharp end of her sword.

In the early 1900s, Wheeler worked as a mountain surveyor in an area called Glacier, now known as Rogers Pass, in British Columbia. Partly for his job and possibly more so for fun, Arthur loved to explore the mountains. His was an office of endless ridge tops, snow-capped peaks, and glacier-fed blue-green lakes. It was not the average work place in the early 1900s — or today for that matter.

While Wheeler explored the peaks in Canada, a fellow climber named Charles Fay was exploring ways to build upon a mountaineering club he had started in the United States. Fay was fixed on the idea of adding a Canadian branch to his newly formed American Alpine

Club. He thought Canada would be fairly represented if the club's name were changed to The Alpine Club of North America. What he did not know was that an influential and very Canadian Elizabeth Parker would challenge such a proposal. She reacted strongly to the suggestion. Why should Canadians be a part of someone else's club when they could form a club of their own?

Since she had never actually climbed to the peak of a mountain, it was not Elizabeth's drive as a mountaineer that got her involved in the discussion. It was her job. Her boss, the editor of the *Manitoba Free Press*, asked Elizabeth to reply to a letter sent to the paper, a letter signed by a Mr. A. O. Wheeler. The letter was a simple request, or so Wheeler had intended, for support from the leading Canadian newspapers to help sell Fay's idea of a Canadian branch of the American Alpine Club. Wheeler had no idea what he was in store for when Elizabeth caught wind of his and Fay's plan.

Elizabeth's response argued completely against the idea of joining an American club. Her passion for Canada's mountains filled the page with phrases such as, "It knocks me speechless and fills me with shame for young Canada," "protest against Alpine organization on any such basis," and "Surely, between Halifax and Victoria, there can be found at least a dozen persons who are made of the stuff needed to climb, and care enough about our mountain heritage." In her true fashion, Elizabeth held back nothing to make her point of view clear. It was time for Canadians to stand on their own two feet and start a club of their own. She signed her response simply, "M.T." (the initials of her mother's maiden name).

Now it was Wheeler's turn to be stunned. First his temper, then his interest in starting a Canadian club were sparked by Elizabeth's sharp words. He felt compelled to respond. Another letter was dropped in the mail, this time addressed directly to M.T. He had no idea that the "Dear Sir" he addressed his letter to was a woman. This was how correspondence between Elizabeth and Wheeler began and before they knew it, they had the ball rolling — the Alpine Club of Canada was about to be born. By 1906, it was official! Canada was home to its own mountaineering club, and people across the country were invited to join.

The late 1800s and early 1900s were a time of firsts in the Rockies. The Alpine Club of Canada was the first mountaineering club that allowed ladies to become members. In its first year, 310 people joined the Club. Seventy-seven of them were women. Within 10 years, the ladies would account for half the Club's membership. The Club's first general mountaineering camp was held in 1906, beginning a summer camp tradition that

Members of the Alpine Club of Canada. Elizabeth Parker, with climbing rope slung over her shoulder, is standing on the front row.

continues today. Women wore dresses to climb at that first camp, but eventually traded their long hems for knickers as was suggested by the guides. After all, as one man said of his wife, who was dressed in *his* clothes, for climbing, "even the shortest skirt maybe might be inconvenient or even dangerous!"

The original intent of the Alpine Club of Canada camps was to promote climbing and mountaineering recreation among Canadians. Unfortunately, in those early years, only the middle and upper class professionals could afford to attend. As travel became less costly with the development of the road network, more Canadians were able to reach the Rockies. Today, almost 100 years since the camp began, nearly 10,000 people have donned crampons, roped up, and climbed countless peaks during the Alpine Club of Canada summer camps. To top it off, by the year 2000, club membership sat at more than 5000 avid mountaineers nationwide.

Poor health began to limit Elizabeth's participation in Alpine Club outings. After the summer of 1913, she could no longer attend the annual camps. Instead, she continued to "educate Canadians about their mountains" with her newspaper columns. Another way she shared her passion for the hills was through her daughter, Jean Parker. Jean had three successful climbing seasons from 1906 to 1909, reaching the top of almost a dozen major peaks in the Rocky and Selkirk Mountains. But after 1913, she too stopped attending the Alpine Club camps, possibly to care for her mother. Back home in Winnipeg, mother and daughter kept in tune with the climbing world by opening their door to local club members or visiting mountaineers.

Elizabeth Parker died in the fall of 1944. She was 88 years old. The Alpine Club of Canada was 38. The old-timers who knew and loved her in the early days of the Club deeply mourned her absence. As Arthur Wheeler said, she was one of the Alpine Club of Canada's most loyal supporters "from the date of that momentous letter bearing the initials 'M.T.'" to the day she died.

Luckily, for the modern mountaineer, the memory of Elizabeth Parker lives on. There is a hut near Lake O'Hara in the Canadian Rockies that bears her name. Back in 1931, when the Alpine Club of Canada wished to pay tribute to Elizabeth Parker by naming this log cabin in her honour, she humbly suggested it be called the Winnipeg Hut instead. No one listened. It was named the Elizabeth Parker Hut, and it remains the flagship of the Alpine Club of Canada's fleet of backcountry huts. Whether the hut is laden with a blanket of snow, or surrounded by a meadow of wildflowers, its charm is difficult to match.

## *Chapter 5*
# Buckskin and Breeches
## Caroline Hinman (1884–1966)

aroline Hinman was the first to admit she had a one-track mind. Travelling filled her every thought. She fuelled her soul in the desert sands of the Sahara, on the waters of the Black Sea Riviera, and throughout the alpine meadows of the Himalayas. Each far-away place fed her dreams and was a springboard to her next adventure. India, the far North, South America — Caroline explored every corner of the Earth. The world was her oyster and the Canadian Rocky Mountains were her pearl.

It was not until 1906, the year Caroline turned 22, that she truly yearned to travel. She had been invited to

California to be a bridesmaid at a friend's wedding. She sent a message that she was on her way and prepared to leave the college classrooms she had sat in for the past four years.

In those days, a person could not simply hop on an airplane and fly across the country in a few hours. Travelling was quite an undertaking. Caroline journeyed by rail car for several days from her home in New Jersey to the beaches, palm trees, and sunny skies of California. Once there, she spent three months in the sunny state, and another two slowly making her way home, stopping to camp along the way. The journey whet her appetite — anything to do with travelling, and especially camping, completely absorbed Caroline for the rest of her days.

However, Caroline's father would not let her slip into the life of a traveller that easily. He advised Caroline to pursue a profession. Yet he did not want to completely deter his daughter from her wandering ways. His solution was to send Caroline to Europe on a guided holiday, but on one condition. Caroline was to pay attention to the guide's methods of running the eight-person tour. Maybe she would like to become a professional tour guide herself? The trip was a huge success, and afterwards two things were very clear: Caroline was destined to travel, and she would love to be a guide. The year was 1909.

Caroline was somewhat of a rarity in the early years of the 20th century. While other women were making their way in the workforce as clerks, typists, and shop assistants, Caroline was planning adventures for would-be clients. Her first venture was a return trip to Europe — only this time she was in charge. She escorted four friends on a career-defining trip, which, unpredictably, coincided with the start of World War I. This turn of events dramatically altered the group's travel plans and the five ladies were stuck in Europe well past their scheduled return date.

Eventually Caroline made it home to the United States, and the trip was considered a big success. Due to the outbreak of the war though, she was forced to put a hold on her newfound career. But she wasn't thwarted. Canada was still a safe place to travel. Caroline bought herself a train ticket and headed northwest. There, for the first time, she laid eyes upon the Canadian Rocky Mountains. It was love at first sight.

\* \* \*

Since the Alpine Club of Canada was formed in 1906, it has run week-long mountaineering camps in Western Canada. During these camps, participants learn mountaineering and ice climbing skills, and they climb as

Caroline Hinman at Mt. Robson, in the mountains she loved

many peaks as possible under the care of mountain guides hired by the club. Caroline attended one of these camps in 1913. This was the same year that Elizabeth Parker, the driving force behind the Alpine Club of Canada, bid the camp a final farewell due to her failing health. Much to Elizabeth Parker's delight, Caroline later held the Alpine Club entirely responsible for triggering her love affair with the Rockies.

The thrill of being at the camp that summer redirected Caroline's life. Her spirits were high and she felt such joy camping among the "glorious mountains." She knew instantly she would have to return to the Rockies. She planned her next trip so that she could resume her adventure tour guiding business and bring guests to the Canadian West. Her new mission in life was to introduce others to the "wonderland of unpolluted air, warm sunshine and brilliant flowers — the land of the spruce, the rock, and the snow."

Hardly six months had passed since her own introduction to the mountains and Caroline was busy mapping out a vacation for six girls for the following summer. An equipment list was drawn up — buckskin jacket, woollen riding breeches or knickers, laced tramping boots with nails in the soles — and menus were planned. Although Caroline organized the trips, and paid attention to every detail, she was not considered the "guide." Instead, she left the guiding to Curly Phillips, a fellow she hired for most of her outings. Several other men were also hired to set up camps along the way and cook for the group. So it was for the summer of 1914 that guides were hired and saddle horses were arranged. Train tickets were purchased and bags were packed. The "little band of girls" would travel by rail car across the continent from the eastern United States to Banff, Alberta where they would say goodbye to their city ways and plunge into the mountain wilderness.

Once again, the reality lived up to the hype. The girls' parents were completely "overjoyed with the health, energy, and bounding spirits which their daughters brought back from the mysterious land of mountains." Without hesitation, they asked Caroline to run a similar trip the next year. So she did — with even more adventure-seekers added to her roster, and again the trip was a great success.

Even though the 1910s saw an emboldening of women — they cut their hair short, began wearing knee-length skirts and, most shocking of all, smoked cigarettes and wore makeup in public — in many ways, Caroline was ahead of her time. It would be another 20 years after Caroline first visited the Rockies that hiking would become a popular pastime. Add a few more years on to that, and women were only just beginning to wear pants in the city centres.

Caroline named her adventure company *Off the Beaten Path* after the motto by which she led her life. For more than 40 years, she offered trips that exposed people of all ages to the Canadian Rockies. Return guests and newcomers alike would join Caroline on one- or two-month expeditions in the mountains. They rode horseback along hidden trails, fished in glacier-fed rivers, hiked up unnamed peaks, and slept in tents perched high above the vast valleys below.

It was the tent sites that earned Caroline the nickname Timberline Kate. She was always seeking out a camping spot high up the mountainside above the tree line. That often made things difficult: the sites were more exposed to wind, water was hard to find, and firewood was scarce. Caroline considered such places beyond compare. She loved the beauty and openness of the grassy meadows, and felt deeply inspired by the views. Above all, she loved sleeping under a wide-open sky and a blanket of stars.

An especially memorable trip was made during the summer of 1921. The adventure was to begin on July 20 in Jasper, Alberta. For 44 days, the party would travel by horseback along countless rivers and over numerous rocky passes, exploring the wilds as they went. This year, before they even hit the trail, the group was delayed a day due to a serious problem. The starting point of the trip, the Stoney River, was in flood.

The fast-flowing waters of the river were impossible to wade through, not only for the guests, but also for the horses. The swift current could have swept even the largest of animals away to their deaths. With 47 horses and 2270 kilograms of gear to transport, the group had only one choice: to ride a freight train across a bridge over the raging river. Quickly everything was reorganized, unpacked, and repacked just in time to catch the evening train that would see them safely across the torrent. Under a full moon, the tired party of 12 was finally deposited onto dry ground on the far side of the Stoney River. Their trip had only just begun.

The journey unfolded as the group skirted the shorelines of lakes and crossed alpine meadows filled with wildflowers, stopping each night at campsites along the route. One day, the group, mounted on their horses, rounded a corner and came within a stone's throw of a huge grizzly bear. Fortunately, the bear was engrossed in digging for gophers and did not notice the group approach. Silently, they watched as the bear excavated large clods of dirt and rocks with his massive paws. He was intent on finding himself a meal! Not sure what to do, but painfully aware of how fragile they felt

Caroline Hinman off the beaten path — her
(and the dog's) favourite place

next to this powerful beast, the group prayed that the
bear would not be alarmed when he turned their way.
They waited. No one wanted to hear the fact that a bear
could outrun a horse. They waited some more. Finally

the bear looked up, confused by his audience of horses and humans, and in a heartbeat, took off. The strength and power of his gait were enough to send a chill up each person's back.

Fear rivaled excitement on the day when two members of the party fell into a crevasse and disappeared into the icy depths of a glacier. The adventure began when Caroline and four others attempted to reach the summit of Mount Chown. Despite hints of sunshine earlier in the day, the weather had turned foul by mid-afternoon. Blinding snow and howling winds caused the group to abandon the climb and head back to camp. The peak would have been too dangerous to climb under such conditions.

The party, however, still had to descend the glacier they had climbed in the morning and now visibility was almost nil. The steep, frozen slope was covered with crevasses, and the threat of falling into the ice-cold cracks was ever present. It was like walking through a minefield, not knowing when danger would strike. The climbers double-checked that the rope tied around their waists — their lifeline — was secure, and then slowly started their descent, ice axes held ready for action. They hoped their guide, Curly Phillips, knew a safe way down.

Not even 15 minutes after the group turned their

back to the peak of Mount Chown, Phillips disappeared. The rope that linked everyone together snapped tight. Their guide had fallen into a crevasse. "Anchor for your lives!" cried Richard Day, second in line to the gaping hole. Ice axes were dug deep into the snow and everybody braced against the pull of the rope. Dangling in the depths of the earth, a suspended Phillips let out a muffled plea, "Give me slack. You are cutting me in two."

With some creative thinking and hefty hauling by the rest of the group, Phillips inched his way out of the crevasse. He was breathless and had a broken rib, but everyone was overjoyed to see him standing. The sky cleared slightly as if to commend the swift rescue. There was no time to lollygag though, and in an instant their celebration was cut short. The storm raged and they were again engulfed in whiteout conditions. Blindly, they proceeded down the glacier.

Another 20 minutes passed before danger struck again. Out of nowhere, the snow-covered ice suddenly split in two. On one side of the wide abyss stood Phillips and Day; on the other Caroline and a Mr. O'Brien; hanging in between was a young girl named Olga Merck. It took some careful maneuvering, but Phillips and Day were able to slowly pull Olga out. The only problem was that Caroline and O'Brien were stranded on the other side of the chasm.

With much consideration and a whole lot of testing the strength of snow bridges with ice axes, a plan was made. In the end, Caroline and O'Brien crossed the crevasse by lying flat on their stomachs over the most sturdy-looking snow bridge they could find, and the rest of the group pulled them to safety.

Finally, the weather cleared enough for the weary mountaineers to find their way home. Before they knew it, the howling storm was a distant memory and they were rejoicing around a roaring campfire and enjoying hot food. As Caroline herself said, "It is the danger and the excitement of mountain climbing that helps make it so interesting, and surely it is the contrast from the cold, snowy glaciers, with their treacherous crevasses that makes camp in the friendly timber seem like the most comfortable home on earth."

To Caroline, summers were meant to be spent in the Rockies. That left the winter months open to explore the rest of the world — and Caroline and Off the Beaten Track were there to make that happen. She organized trips to Northern Algeria, Tunisia, Sicily and Naples; the Panama Canal, Guatemala, and Southern California; and the tropical islands of Ceylon, Sumatra, and Java. Caroline and her guests travelled by steamship, houseboat, and canoe; on foot and camelback; and by caravan. No boundary was set on how the group would get to such out-of-the-way places. In a single day, they would stare breathless at the striking contrast between mountain-view and desert. They would revel in the beauty of the tropics. Their experiences were endless. There was no hill unclimbed on a trip when travelling with Caroline.

A world traveller by trade, and certainly by choice, Caroline Hinman was a person who never suffered from boredom. How could she — she was always either on a trip or busy planning the next one. Her love for the wilderness was so powerful she had to share it with others. She introduced hundreds of newcomers to the mountains. Thanks to her, women could let down their hair, get their fingernails dirty and put etiquette class on hold. Instead of needlepoint and knitting, they rode "the trails of the Rocky Mountains ... camped in hidden valleys and at high passes ... slept in Indian tepees at 15 below zero and saw the mountain world in the dazzling beauty of heavy snow."

Yet, when she looked back over the years, she humbly wondered where the time had gone. With no husband, no children, no home of her own, no books written, and no fortune to pass on, Caroline felt she had accomplished very little. However, she also had no regrets. She had broken all conventions of the era by following her heart and leading the life to which she had been drawn. Caroline loved her job and there was no place she would have rather been than exploring places off the beaten track.

## Chapter 6
# Boundless
## Georgia Engelhard (1906–1986)

eorgia Engelhard was an explorer who linked two eras. Her lifespan connected the early days of mountaineering to the modern climbing scene. In the 1930s, she laid claim to 32 first ascents in the Canadian West, an extraordinary feat for a climber, male or female! By the 1980s, she was witness to the breakthrough of women making bold ascents up big peaks all over the world.

Like many mountaineers before her, and many more to come, Georgia fell in love with the Canadian Rockies. The towering walls of limestone were a welcomed pleasure far removed from the skyline of tall buildings that encircled her home in New York City. Her love for the mountains, however, was slow to form. When she visited the Alps and the Dolomites in Europe as a young girl, she was somewhat reserved. The peaks were "handsome" she thought, but mountain climbing was simply "an insane sport." More excited about horseback riding, Georgia had no ambition to climb. Besides, she was scared of heights.

Born of a well-to-do family, Georgia was exposed to the mountains on several family holidays. Eventually, a trip to Lake Louise changed her feelings about the rugged peaks. It was the summer of 1926, and Georgia was somehow persuaded to try rock climbing. Much to her surprise, she loved it! Suddenly the surrounding mountains, glaciers, and trails had new meaning for the excited 20 year-old. She became so enraptured by climbing, that spending time with her parents became second choice. For the next 15 years, Georgia returned to the Rockies every summer to conquer as many peaks as possible. There was no mention of horseback riding again.

* * *

On the east shore of Lake Louise sits a hotel referred to as the "Diamond of the Wilderness." Today, it is an enormous four-season, five-star chateau. In 1890, the original building was a small wooden structure with a veranda, sitting room, and bedroom. Its sole purpose was to house the outdoor adventurer and alpinist. Twelve guests could comfortably call it home. By the early 1900s, the number of visitors passing through the area of Lake Louise increased to an astonishing 5,000 people. It was time for an expansion. A concrete and half-timbered wing was added to the hotel, and by the time Georgia arrived in the summer of 1926, another addition had been built — eight more stories of decorative brick. This became known as the Chateau Lake Louise. It was a friendly place, not overcrowded, and to Georgia it seemed more like a country club than a hotel. More importantly, it allowed the budding mountaineer to rub shoulders with some of the great climbers of the time.

On one particular occasion, Georgia built up the courage to approach Cora Best, the prominent lady mountaineer of the day. Cora just had returned from climbing Mount Victoria, the 3464-metre peak that fills the view from the hotel's great windows. In a brave voice, Georgia said she hoped to climb this mountain one day. A "snooty" Miss Best responded: "Young woman, that is an ambition that will take many years to fulfill." Ha! Georgia reached the summit of Victoria the following summer. By the time her days in the Rockies

Georgia Englehard — always ready to
climb with ice axe in hand

came to an end, Georgia had climbed the mountain 13 times.

Within a few years of her first visit to Lake Louise, Georgia had already begun to make a name for herself as a mountaineer. In 1929, she climbed nine peaks in nine days — each summit standing well above the 3000-metre mark. On the day after she climbed the ninth peak, the same day she was to head home to New York, Georgia awoke in the wee hours of the morning. A full moon spread a silver light upon the lake and the glaciers beyond. She rose early, and in her usual tireless fashion, she bounded up a nearby pathway to the top of Mount St. Piran. The two-hour burst of energy was exactly what she needed before sitting in a train for days.

High above the shadowed Lake Louise, Georgia basked in her happiness. The peaks that surrounded her, all of which she had climbed, "were bathed in golden, rosy light." As she gazed at the breathtaking view, the youthful climber was struck by a sensation she would never forget — the realization of how extremely small a person is in the company of these majestic mountains.

By the 1930s, dainty flowers, polka dots, and stripes were the fashion. Movies had become the greatest influence on clothing, and Hollywood was predicted to replace New York City as North America's fashion centre. Meanwhile, Georgia was making her own fashion statement. With her slender frame, boldly cropped hair, and fly-front pants she looked more like a teenage boy than a well-to-do lady. It was a style that was well suited for the mountains, but it had got her thrown out of many a lady's room and beer parlor. Even at the age of 30, she was often mistaken for a young lad.

Georgia had her own brush with Hollywood in 1931. She starred in a movie called "She Climbs to Conquer." The experience involved climbing Mount Victoria seven times in a row, and then being chased from the peak by a death-defying lightening storm on the final day of filming. Thunder "boomed back and forth from the rock walls" and flames exploded as lightening struck the mountainside. Georgia's nailed boots and steel-headed ice axe hummed with the vibration of electricity in the air. She was intent on reaching the hut at Abbot's Pass for safety. It was quite possibly one of the fastest descents down Mount Victoria.

That same summer proved to be one of Georgia's most successful visits to Canada — she completed 38 mountain ascents in one season! It was a record she would increase to 40 ascents in 1936. One of her guides claimed she climbed more peaks than he did in all his days of climbing. Another summed up Georgia's display of drive by saying (in his strong Swiss accent), "Dat Georgia, she vants to do too much!"

Not everyone was impressed by a woman's accomplishments in the mountains, as Georgia discovered after an ascent on Mount Hungabee. Georgia and her guide, Ernest Feuz, tackled a long route up the north face of the peak, a route that had only been climbed twice before. The two climbers reached the summit in only five hours — despite a pitch they described as having no foot- or handholds. (To reach a far-off hold Ernest stood on Georgia's back, then her shoulders, and then her head! Georgia's comment: "Even with my thick hair and a hat the bite of those boot nails was anything but comfortable.") They made it to the top of the mountain just as another guide, Rudolph Aemmer, and his client arrived via the standard route. As mountaineering etiquette dictates, Rudolph was invited to descend first with his client since he was the more senior guide. Georgia and Ernest followed but the pace was painfully slow. Finally, having lost patience, Georgia and Ernest excused themselves and sped by. They were settled in camp sipping tea by the time the second pair crept in two hours later. Rudolph's client was outraged! A girl had beaten him both up and down the mountain! "It should not be allowed!" he exploded at the camp manager. With a smirk, the manager, who was a woman, responded that there was nothing she could do.

\* \* \*

"Adventure in the mountains is a sign of inefficiency," reads an old quote. Georgia admired these words. She agreed that adventure meant mishap and she was proud to claim she had none. Georgia certainly had her close calls, though. On one climb, it was sheer luck that the extra 15 minutes it took to brew a cup of coffee saved her life.

Georgia's adventure occurred on the descent from Mount Victoria in 1936. She was climbing with her future husband, Oliver Eaton Cromwell. Tony, as she called him, was an experienced mountaineer, and shared every bit of Georgia's passion for the rugged peaks. Much to the disgust of one of Georgia's long-time guides, Tony and Georgia chose never to hire mountain guides once they began climbing together. The pair was about to complete the traverse of Mount Victoria from its north to south end, a first without the expertise of a guide.

They were at Abbot's Pass and about to descend a steep, narrow passage on Victoria Glacier. There were sheer cliffs of rock on either side of the gully, and above lay gigantic masses of ice. Avalanches would threaten their every step. Known as The Death Trap, the passage is not a place to dawdle. The couple would have to be fast. As they were planning their descent, a blood-curdling crack echoed all around them. A mix of rock and ice "thundered and hurtled" past them through the gully. If not for the 15-minute brew they had allowed at Abbot's Pass, Georgia and Tony would have been trapped in the avalanche zone. They would have been killed in an instant.

* * *

There was another side to Georgia — the photographer. By the mid-1940s, people other than climbers were enthralled with stories about mountain adventure. Since a picture is worth a thousand words, mountain photography was in demand. Georgia had snapped her fair share of 'bum' shots while climbing (looking up to snap a quick photo of the climber above her), but she quickly realized that for the professional look she would have to stage photo sessions in the mountains. The bulky camera equipment of the day made it too difficult for Georgia to enjoy a climb while taking photographs. So in 1945, she became a professional photographer and focused on her subjects rather than the climb. Even in the modern day, a person who earns a living from taking pictures is a rare find. Back then, it added to Georgia's pioneering flare.

From the Matterhorn in Switzerland to Canada's Matterhorn, Mount Assiniboine, Georgia built her collection of stunning black and white mountain images. The magazine world wanted photos that said, "You can do it, too!" Georgia fulfilled the request: a climber leaping across a crevasse on a glacier, a mountain guide pounding in a piton on a steep rock face, and two team members sharing the customary handshake on top of a mountain peak. She captured the precision and mystique of climbing that fed people's dreams. Each of her photos was worth $7.50 to the *Toronto Star Weekly* — at the time, that was 50 cents more than the daily rate paid to hire a mountain guide.

Georgia was a pioneer in another sense — she married Tony Cromwell at the age of 41 (a late age by anyone's standards in those days). Georgia and Tony continued a life of adventure, moving to Switzerland and filling their winters with skiing, their summers with climbing and photography. The couple never returned to Canada. Georgia knew it would be too different from her first days there. Already by the mid-1930s, she had seen the "ambience" of Lake Louse vanish with the flood of tourists. In her later years, she simply wished to "cherish" her "illusions" of the Canadian Rockies.

Georgia Engelhard-Cromwell died in 1986 — the same year that Sharon Wood reached the summit of

Mount Everest. Georgia was a passionate mountain explorer. Her spirit stands as tall as the peak that bears her name: Engelhard Tower, on Mount Murchison, in Banff National Park.

# Chapter 7
# Soul Explorer
## Leanne Allison (1969– )

n the evening of April 20, 2003, Leanne Allison had just finished eating another one-pot meal — this time, turkey and mashed potatoes. It was Easter, after all. No matter what the occasion though, each meal turned out the same — like mush. Given her whereabouts, that was to be expected. She was deep in the wilderness. Again.

One hundred years have passed since women explorers, in search of hidden trails and unclimbed peaks, first set foot in the western Canadian mountains. Now it is up to modern-day adventurers, like Leanne, to carry the torch. But in this day and age, when people flock to the wilderness in droves, there is an entirely new motivation for adventure — to bring awareness to what could be lost. This is an era when care for the environment is critical. For Leanne, preservation of nature is what gives meaning to her life as an explorer.

Leanne grew up in Calgary, Alberta, but it was on Long Beach in British Columbia where she first felt privy to the elements. Barely a toddler then, she battled against the strong winds that blew in with the tide off the Pacific Ocean. Her parents had to hold her hands for fear that their little girl would get blown away. For Leanne, the experience was pure fun. She loved it, and deep down inside, a seed was planted: her future would be spent in the great outdoors.

The Rocky Mountains were (and still are) one of Leanne's favourite playgrounds. As a child, she spent many a day hiking the wooded trails and stony peaks with her family. At 10 years of age she announced in a confident manner that she was ready for summer camp. Off she went. Like everything else outdoors, she loved it, and to no one's surprise was named "camper of the week." When her parents picked Leanne up from the bus at the end of camp, they asked if she had missed them. She had to admit that they had not even crossed her mind!

Leanne was so captivated with her camp experience

that she spent her teen years as a camp counsellor. She had the good fortune of working with like-minded women who fuelled her spirit even more. They told her about the Outdoor Pursuits program at The University of Calgary. What a perfect match — education with an outdoor slant. "Sign me up!" The enthusiastic 17 year-old found herself enrolled in the program before she even knew how to use a carabiner. This modern-day explorer was on her way.

During the next few years Leanne soaked up every mountain sport she could — climbing, backpacking, mountaineering, skiing, and paddling. She left nothing untried, and set her mind to master every activity. After school and before the responsibility of a "real" job took hold, Leanne did what many educated, prospering 20 year olds do. She became a ski bum. Her parents could hardly complain. After all, she was simply fine-tuning the skills she had learned in school. Besides, adventure had become a solid fixture in Leanne's life. Ski bumming was part of the journey.

While Leanne was skiing powder, a friend of hers, Karsten Heuer, was studying the effect that developments — such as ski areas — had on wildlife in the Bow Valley of Banff National Park. During his four-winter study, it became all too obvious that the movements of wolves, cougars, lynxes, and wolverines were being

Leanne enjoying the beauty of the wilderness — even
with a heavy load on her back

blocked by land developments. The continuous building of houses, hotels, roads, and golf courses were making it impossible for animals to roam freely through
their natural habitats.

Karsten believed major steps had to be taken to
preserve the wildlife.

Not many women can say they met their husband
in Kindergarten, but Leanne can. Karsten was her first
boyfriend. As cute as it was to have a commitment of the
heart at age five, the early romance did not last. As fate
would have it, however, the pair met again in university.
They were reintroduced when a friend of Leanne's said,
"He's the male version of you!"

Indeed he was. There was an instant attraction, and
suddenly Leanne had a companion who would share
mountain adventures with her. One trip she will never
forget was their ski ascent up Mount Rhonda on the
Wapta Icefield. It was Karsten's first ski trip on a glacier.
Tied into a rope for safety, the team travelled in unison.
At the end of the climb, when it was time to descend the
glacier, Leanne pointed her skis and took off down the
north face. She skied from top to bottom non-stop. Still
attached to the rope, Karsten's screams trailed behind
her. His thighs burned with tired muscles! Leanne gave
him no choice but to stay upright and ski. He dumped
her not long after.

Although they went their separate ways for a while, Leanne and Karsten still shared many outdoor trips. It is not easy to find a compatible partner for the mountains, so in love or not, they remained good friends.

As the years passed, Karsten became an explorer in his own right. He completed expeditions across some of North America's most remote and rugged land — for the sake of endangered wildlife. His adventures are, in a word, epic. One epic — a hike from Yellowstone National Park in Wyoming to Watson Lake in the Yukon Territory — altered the course of Karsten's life. When he invited Leanne to join him for part of it, her life took a 90-degree turn as well.

The trip was an ambitious 3400-kilometre journey along the spine of the Rocky Mountains. Karsten would travel the entire distance with one purpose in mind — to see what challenges wildlife faced with the increase of human activity in the region.

This hike was part of a bigger vision — the Yellowstone to Yukon Conservation Initiative, or Y2Y for short. The idea of Y2Y is to create wildlife movement corridors that link existing parks and protected lands. These corridors will allow animals such as grizzly bears, lynxes, and wolves to safely roam from one protected area to another without the risk of encountering such artificial obstructions as highways. Nothing is more difficult or dangerous for a bear than crossing a highway. The Y2Y corridor theory looked good on paper. Karsten wanted to be sure it would work for the animals.

When he began his trek in the summer of 1998, Karsten and Leanne were not together. Leanne was on a journey of her own in Vancouver, British Columbia. She had accomplished a lot since her ski bum days, having studied glaciers in Antarctica, then avalanches in Blue River, British Columbia. She had also reached the summit of Mount Logan. At 5959 metres Mount Logan is the highest peak in Canada, and the second highest in North America. With a base measuring 50 kilometres from one side to the other, it is also one of the largest mountains by mass in the world. Mount Logan sits majestically in the St. Elias Range in the Yukon. The St. Elias area is extremely remote, and in the early days the only way to access it was on foot. That meant a 1500-kilometre walk to the base of Mount Logan. As a result, it took three major expeditions — a reconnaissance mission, the freighting of supplies, and finally a push to the summit — to complete the first ascent of the mountain in 1925.

In 1993, Leanne and three other women set out to accomplish another first on Mount Logan. They would be the first all-female team to reach the east summit via the East Ridge, a technical and demanding route up the mountain. Compared to the thousands of kilograms of cargo that the 1925 team required in their day, Leanne and her teammates would pack no more than 25 kilograms on their backs. Food and stove fuel for a month, tents, and climbing gear were all they needed. The modern-day ski-plane flight to the base of the mountain certainly made logistics easier!

The team of women endured three weeks on Mount Logan only to spend moments on the summit. It was too cold to hang around, and the comfort and security of their tents at Base Camp was beckoning. Mission accomplished, they set their sights on home, unaware of the excitement yet to come.

After two days of descending the mountain, Base Camp stood a mere 300 metres away. Leanne, Andrea Petzold, Mary Clayton, and Sylvia Forest had survived steep snow and ice sections, bad weather, and cramped quarters higher on the mountain. The homestretch was a welcomed sight. Then, with a loud crash, a massive piece of ice suddenly broke from the hanging glacier above, sending a torrent of ice and snow down the mountainside to the valley below. Their Base Camp was right in its path. The climbers stood breathless, and watched as the avalanche — by far the biggest any of them had ever seen — engulfed their tents. Panicked thoughts of "What if we were farther down the mountain?" flooded their minds. It was difficult to feel safe any longer, but as luck would have it, the camp narrowly escaped burial. The women breathed a sigh of relief.

After Mount Logan and the Antarctic, the lush green and warmth of her new home on the west coast felt like paradise. Leanne welcomed the change with open arms. She was on a new path. Yoga became her passion. Paddling was her play. The call of the wild was not at the top of her priority list — except for the fact that Karsten had put a bug in her ear before he set foot on the Y2Y trail.

Would Leanne join Karsten on the second half of the trip? A month-long ski traverse, 43 days of hiking, and a two-week canoe trip that connected Jasper to the Yukon. Interested? Leanne knew the two of them traveled well together, and they trusted and respected each other's abilities in the mountains. This trip had purpose, and Leanne was intrigued by what she would learn from living in the wilderness for that length of time. How could she resist?

Along with another friend, Jay Honeyman, they would set out the following spring on skis. After that, Leanne and Karsten would continue the trek together. In the meantime, Karsten would complete the first half of the trip with his trusty canine companion — Webster.

After months of preparation and anticipation, it took only 15 minutes for the three skiers to leave behind the hustle and bustle of city life. Their world was now this: winter in the wilderness, each other, and the 450 untracked kilometres that lay ahead.

At 30 kilograms (70 pounds), Leanne's pack was heavy and she severely doubted her ability to finish the trip. She longed for a warm room and a moment to practice yoga. And it was only day three of the trip.

Thankfully, the human body adapts, and as the days passed, Leanne's body adjusted to the demands of the expedition. But her mind still needed to adjust, she needed to be rid of the negative thoughts that so easily slipped in. On a sunny afternoon, Leanne found a quiet place to practice yoga. It was not the room she had been dreaming about since the start of the trip, but it was warm.

The sun cast a spell of relaxation as she moved from one yoga pose to another on a flat spot in the snow. And then in a flash the words of a fellow yoga teacher came to her: *Accept the work ahead and do it.* Leanne embraced the simple notion. She let down her guard and accepted the weight of the heavy pack, accepted the miles of skiing to come. As a result, she felt renewed, and her days were filled with a calm steadiness. This stillness within was what had been missing on the ski trip so far, and perhaps on all her adventures. This fresh state of mind would be the foundation for adventures to come.

Leanne's newfound source of strength did not change the hardships that the team encountered — there were still dangerous avalanche slopes to cross, mazes of frozen waterfalls to navigate, and deep heavy snow to break trail through. However, her approach was quite different now when it came to managing the terrain. She was learning to *be* one with the environment, like the wolverine they had followed for three days. The animal's route had led them up and around sections in the valley that were otherwise impassable. The wolverine knew the terrain and they trusted it. "The spacing between the tracks told a story of how it loped along at a steady pace and never wavered off course for rest, food, or water. It was a pattern of raw determination and focus." That same pattern guided the skiers for the remainder of their trip.

Six weeks after they hung up their skis, Leanne and Karsten were right back where they left off. This time they would complete the final stretch of the Y2Y expedition. With spring in the air, the challenges of the previous leg were all but forgotten. Challenges such as the heavy snowfall that slowed their progress to an annoying five kilometres a day instead of their usual 15. Or the night when their sleeping bags offered nothing but a place to shiver because they were so soggy and wet from the snow that seeped in through their packs. Or the final 40 kilometers that turned into a two-day walk on a logging road instead of a pleasant ski. Each memory slipped away. Leanne was on a new section of the journey with a fresh set of hardships to endure. She had room for only one thought in her mind: Accept the work ahead.

Leanne and Karsten plunged their canoe into the ice-cold Murray River at the base of Kinuseo Falls, more than 1200 kilometres from their destination. The river was in full spring flood. The thundering waterfall did not help create a sense of calm in the strong current, but as the rhythm of their paddling stroke picked up and the river mellowed, Leanne, Karsten, and Webster were happy to be on their way.

Five days later, they swapped lifejackets for backpacks and hit the trail. Swarms of mosquitoes and flies attacked them as soon as they were on foot. Leanne and Karsten donned headnets, tightened pant cuffs, and tucked in long, thick-sleeved shirts. They promptly overheated, but the bugs were relentless as they squeezed far enough through the fine mesh of the headnets to draw blood. Not a layer of clothing could be shed. Poor Webster.

*Soul Explorer*

So began 43 days of walking through the largest area in British Columbia that is without roads. To reach their goal, they would encounter dangerous river crossings, electrical storms, and bears. Their route along the northern Rocky Mountains had hardly been touched by anyone else on foot, and only a few people knew the country well enough to offer some advice. Basically, they were alone. Leanne's only choice was to accept the situation. *Accept the work ahead and do it.*

What fuels an explorer? For Leanne it is conservation. Her motivation for adventure has evolved from that of personal achievement to caring deeply for the big picture — nature, the environment, the planet. Her Y2Y experience of living in the wilderness for three months changed her life. For one, she learned to focus on the moment at hand. It would have been easy to feel overwhelmed by the constant unknowns. Is there a river too unsafe to cross? Does that canyon lead to a dead end? Will the food cache still be hanging in the trees when we need it? What if one of us gets injured? The answer for Leanne was to live in the moment — consider her surroundings, assess the situation, and make a decision. Her life depended on it.

She also learned from the behaviour of the animals they encountered: spend energy wisely, rest when possible, drink from every stream. But most importantly, observe. Leanne and Karsten spent long stretches of time staring through binoculars. Much to their amazement, after 5 or 10 minutes of soaking in a scene, an entire herd of elk would appear on a hillside that at first glance looked bare.

It was these experiences that fuelled Leanne to continue her life of exploration — the elk that appeared on the hillside, the wolverine that guided them up a mountain slope, or the odd smell that suggested a bear was nearby. Each connection with nature pushed her forward.

\* \* \*

Once the Y2Y hike was complete, Leanne shifted her focus. First, to making plans for a wedding — her and Karsten's — then to following the porcupine caribou.

Imagine, tens of thousands of caribou flowing across the mountains. Dramas unfolding every minute. Cows calling out for their drowned calves. Calves crying for their lost mothers. Bears giving chase across the tundra. This is Karsten's telling of the caribou migration he saw two summers earlier while on patrol as a park warden in the Yukon's northern Ivvavik National Park. He felt an immediate need to learn more.

Leanne also witnessed a caribou migration. She

Leanne battles the bugs

too was struck by the desire to understand, experience, and document the hardships that the caribou endure. The environmentalist side of her felt the need to protect the endangered calving grounds. The explorer in her had to experience the life of the caribou before she could truly understand what was at risk.

This was how, on a spring day in 2003, Leanne found herself in a familiar situation — a heavy pack slung on her back, skis underfoot, and endless miles of frozen land ahead. With Karsten by her side and a herd of caribou on the move around them, the husband and wife team were already in the depths of their next adventure.

Compared to other trips, this one will be really, *really* gruelling. The trip will involve seven months of skiing and hiking 2000 kilometres across some of the Arctic's most remote tundra. They will follow the porcupine caribou, a herd of more than 120,000, from the outskirts of Old Crow in the Yukon to Alaska's Arctic National Wildlife Refuge, and back. The purpose of their quest is to understand what is at stake if the caribou's calving grounds in the wildlife refuge are opened to oil and gas development. The expedition's name is perfect. It is called *Being Caribou.*

This is a tough trip — their toughest yet. They are tired, cold, and often wet. They travel with the herd for as long as they can each day, only to be left behind when they stop to camp for the night. They drag their leaden limbs out of their frosted sleeping bags each morning to start again, to try to keep up. Meanwhile, the rawness of life and death surrounds them. The herd is in full stampede. Wolf packs wait in ambush as throngs of caribou pass by. Ravens circle above the fresh kill of a yearling. The migration rushes forward.

The couple follows the caribou's tracks into the mountains and onto ever-high ridges. Their path is determined by the course of the caribou. The entire trip is an unknown, except for the fact that by June they will arrive at the herd's summer range where mothers will give birth to their calves.

In the days leading up to their trip, Leanne and Karsten struggled with how to determine when the caribou migration would begin. A friend in Old Crow said, "Listen to your dreams." That night, Leanne dreamt the ice on the Porcupine River was breaking up. They strapped on their skis the next morning, and their adventure began.

# 100 Years of Women and Adventure

In the past 100 years, women have made their names known in the world of mountain adventure. From the early 1900s to the present day, their exploits have proven time and time again that the mountains are a source of strength and vitality. The majestic peaks have opened many a female explorer's hearts, and answered the loftiest of their dreams. To these women, the mountains are their lifeline. Here is a sample from a long list of ladies who have climbed the highest peaks, camped in alpine meadows, or raced down mountain slopes. From wool to Gore-Tex, horseback to mountain bike — the spirit of adventure continues.

1901    Evelyn Berens was the first lady to reach the summit of Mount Sir Donald (3297 metres) in Rogers Pass, one of the most spectacular peaks in Canada. Puzzled by what to wear on the climb, she chose an outfit from her husband's wardrobe

— woollen knickers, puttees, and a collared shirt. "Having been a girl all my life, it was certainly embarrassing, to say the least, suddenly blossoming into a boy." To add to her embarrassment, an enthusiastic crowd greeted Evelyn at the end of the 16-hour climb — with no time for her to change into more lady-like attire.

1904   Gertrude Benham, one of the first serious female mountaineers to visit Canada, arrived in Lake Louise. She spent only one summer in the Rocky and Selkirk Mountains, but climbed more peaks during those few months than some mountaineers do in a lifetime! Several first ascents — including Mount Fay, and first woman to reach the summit of Mount Assiniboine — were highlights of her visit.

1905   The Alpine Club of Canada was formed. Its main objective was to "popularize mountaineering" and encourage Canada to "become a nation of mountaineers." Elizabeth Parker, the driving force behind the Alpine Club of Canada, would be proud — the club still thrives today with more than 5000 members.

1910   The first chocolate bar was created in Canada, and sold for five cents. Not an adventure in itself, but surely a noteworthy addition to the lunch bag of the mountain explorer!

1916   The highest town in Canada (1540 metres) was named Lake Louise. It was first known as Emerald Lake when the area was discovered in 1882. One year later it became the hamlet of Holt City, and then Laggan. Located in Banff National Park, residents have to be employed to live there — Lake Louise ski hill and hotel staff, and abundant wildlife are the main inhabitants of the small town.

1920   Julian May Young retired after 20 years of managing Glacier House in Rogers Pass. For two decades she withstood the isolation and harsh climate of winters in the Selkirk Mountains, all the while leading the hotel to growth and prosperity. Known as Mother Young, she was very popular with the guests and mountain guides. She died in 1925, the same year that Glacier House finally closed its doors to the public.

1924    Phyllis Munday was the first woman to reach the summit of Mount Robson (3954 metres), the highest peak in the Rockies (and long thought to be the highest Canadian peak south of the territories). The next year marked the start of a decade-long quest of exploration and summit attempts on Mount Waddingtion (4016 metres), the true highest peak. Despite her passion and persistence, she never set foot on its summit.

1934    "Georgia Engelhard Champion Mountain Climber Shows How to Increase Your Energy!" read the headline of a full-page comic strip advertisement for the R.J. Reynolds Tobacco Company. The comic depicted Georgia's climb in record time of Mount Victoria. She was shown bounding ahead of her guide, until she fell and needed a lift — from a Camel cigarette. "A Camel picks me up in a few minutes and gives me the energy to push on!" "No smoking" campaigns were years away.

1960    The Icefields Parkway, now one of the world's most scenic highways, was completed from Lake Louise to Jasper. This 230-kilometre stretch of road takes half a day to drive. In the early 1900s, it took Caroline Hinman three weeks to travel the same distance on horseback.

1961   Esther Kafer reached the summit of Mount Waddington, and was the second woman to do so. Her career grew to include numerous first ascents and wilderness exploration, which is quite a feat for a woman who once said, "I don't think we'll ever be able to be that daring and go into the mountains where no one else has been before." One trip included a hike out from the Lillooet Icefield to Pemberton. The expected three-day walk turned into a six-day epic. Desperate measures to reach civilization included chopping down a tree with ice axes in hopes of building a bridge across a raging river. The hikers ended up having to set fire to the tree to make it fall over. When it finally fell, the tree snapped in half and was useless! Esther bushwhacked naked through thick forest in search of a safe way across the river; and the group ran out of food.

1971   Alison Purdey reached the summit of Mount St. Elias, the second highest peak in Canada. The team of eight included Alison and another woman, Marg Wyborn. The mountain had seen

30 attempts and only five ascents prior to this expedition. At Base Camp the team awaited their final drop of food from an airplane before they started the climb. As planned, a Cessna buzzed by, but much to the team members' surprise, dropped only one box onto the glacier. An attached note said "gone fishing" — the Alaska Airlines Terminal had closed early, and the supplies for the mountaineering team were locked indoors.

1975   Junko Tabei, a member of a Japanese expedition, was the first woman to climb Mount Everest.

1977   The first all-women's expedition made a heroic effort on Mount Logan, the highest point in Canada. Team members Kathy Calvert, Lorraine Drewes, Diana Knaak, Cathy Langill, Judy Sterner, and Sharon Wood spent 24 days on skis ascending the King's Trench route. It was a bitter -35° Celsius on summit day. Cold and tired, the team retreated before reaching the summit.

1983   The first all-women's ski traverse was completed from the Bugaboos in the Purcell Mountains to Rogers Pass. Team members were Kathy Calvert,

Sylvia Forest, Lin Heidt, and Martha McCallum. The two-week trip began with a helicopter flying by and dropping cinnamon buns to the four women below. Later in the trip, a grizzly bear and her three cubs greeted the skiers on their descent from Silent Pass. Having no intention of sharing a camp spot with the animals, the team broke into a warden's cabin (much to Kathy's chagrin — she was a warden at the time) for a more peaceful sleep.

1983 The first one-day ski traverse of the Wapta Icefields by an all-woman team was completed. Martha McCallum and Sylvia Forest skied the distance in 11 hours (usually a three-day trip). No rest for the weary — Martha repeated the performance a week later with another friend, Wendy Rockafellow.

1987 At nine years old, Canadian Natalie Renner was the youngest person to climb Mount Assiniboine, the highest peak in the southern Rocky Mountains. Her father, Sepp Renner, a mountain guide and operator of Assiniboine Lodge, promised Natalie one thing if she made it to the top: she would no longer have to guide the "turtles" (slower hikers) who visited the lodge. Excited, she chatted the entire way up the giant mountain. But somewhere along the way, the promise went amiss and Natalie found herself, once again, leading the turtles on summer hikes.

1986    Sharon Wood was the first North American woman to climb Mount Everest.

1989    Lake Louise Ski Area hosted its first women's World Cup in downhill ski racing. The fastest women's downhill speed clocked at the 2002/2003 World Cup race in Lake Louise was 120.33 km/hr!

1992    Diny Harrison became the first fully certified female professional mountain guide in Canada. In 1995, Alison Andrews was the second woman to earn mountain guide status, and Helen Sovdat was third in 1996. Today, there are only seven Canadian fully certified female mountain guides.

1993    The first all-women's team reached the East Summit of Mount Logan via the technical East Ridge. Leanne Allison, Mary Clayton, Sylvia Forest, and Andrea Petzold spent three weeks on

the mountain dealing with freezing temperatures, poor weather conditions, and high avalanche hazard. At times they straddled the knife-
edge ridgeline with nothing but 1000 metres of
open space dropping below them on either side.

1997 Kim Csizmazia, a Canmore, Alberta-based ice
climber, pushed the limits for women on difficult
waterfall ice. She was the first female to climb the
most challenging ice grades of the day. She won
the X Games (the "extreme sport" Olympics) in
1998 and 1999. In 2000, Kim climbed the hardest
mixed climb (ice and rock) in the world, and won
the Ice World Cup. Her words of encouragement
for women in adventure: "You can do whatever
you want. Do it your own way. Figure out what
your strengths are, and do it."

1999 Nancy Greene, a leading downhill skier in her
day, was declared Canada's female athlete of the
20th century. She was a two-time Olympic
medallist (gold in Giant Slalom, and silver in
Slalom) in 1968, and a two-time winner of the
World Cup in 1967 and 1968. Her aggressive skiing style earned her the nickname "The Tiger."
Her insight for adventure: Maintain a real love for

your sport, and "have commitment to work hard and never give up."

2002   Cristina Begy and Meagan Harrod were the top women's team in the first Fernie TransRockies Challenge. Rated the world's most adventurous mountain bike race, the TransRockies Challenge covers 600 kilometres of wilderness trails from Fernie, British Columbia to Canmore, Alberta. Of the 50 teams competing in the week-long event, only four teams were female. Cristina and Meagan finished the race in 39 hours, 30 minutes, and 14 seconds.

2003   Nancy Hansen of Canmore plans to complete her goal of being the first female mountaineer to climb all the 11,000-foot (3353-metre) peaks in the Canadian Rockies. From a tick list of 51 peaks, she has two left to climb, Whitehorn Mountain and Mount Forbes.

# Bibliography

Blake, Don. *Alberta Trivia.* Edmonton, AB: Lone Pine Publishing, 1992.

Bowers, Vivien. *Only in Canada.* Toronto, ON: Maple Tree Press Inc., 2002.

Gillman, Peter. "Everest — Eighty years of triumph and tragedy" in *The Mountaineers.* 2nd Ed., 2000.

Gustole, M. and Gustole, R. *Discovering Canadian Pioneers.* Don Mills, ON: Oxford University Press Canada, 1998.

Heuer, Karsten. *Walking the Big Wild.* Toronto, ON: McClelland & Stewart Ltd., 2002.

Patterson, Bruce. *Canadians on Everest.* Calgary, AB: Detselig Enterprises Ltd., 1990.

Putnam, William. *The Great Glacier and Its House.* New York, NY: The American Alpine Club, Inc., 1982.

Putnam, W., Boles, G., and Laurilla, R. *Place Names of the Canadian Alps*. Revelstoke, B.C.: Footprint Publishing, 1990.

Scott, Chic. *Pushing the Limits*. Calgary, AB: Rocky Mountain Books, 2000.

Smith, Cyndi. *Off the Beaten Track*. Jasper, AB: Coyote Books, 1989.

Wood, Sharon. "Coming Down" in *The Canadian Mountaineering Anthology*. Vancouver, B.C.: Lone Pine Publishing, 1994.

# Web Sites

The Alpine Club of Canada:
www.alpineclubofcanada.ca

The Yellowstone to Yukon Conservation Initiative:
www.y2y.net

# Acknowledgments

There is an old saying that it takes a village to raise a child — the same can be said for writing a book. My sincere thank you to everyone who contributed to the telling of this story.

A special thanks to Leanne Allison and Sharon Wood for sharing your adventures with me. An additional thank you to the women explorers of an earlier era whose lives helped shape this book.

Thank you for your valuable input via handwritten letters, e-mails, and telephone interviews: Nancy Allison, Jane Bateman, Barry Blanchard, Nancy Hansen, Erica Heuer, Heather Swystun, and Cherryl Stea.

Without the staff at the Archives of the Whyte Museum of the Canadian Rockies and the Canmore Public Library, I would still be searching for information. Thank you.

Thanks for your friendly support and kind childcare: Lisa Druckenmiller, Zoe Whalen, and especially, Kathleen Wiebe.

Neil Caldwell and Kirsten Ellingson, and Martha McCallum — thanks for sharing your space.

## Acknowledgments

Thanks to Nancy Mackenzie for your fine editing skills and polished touch, and to Kara Turner and Altitude Publishing for this opportunity to be creative.

Thanks to my family, especially my parents Margaret and Brian Rolfe, and friends who provided tidbits of information and words of encouragement when I needed them most.

And to my love, Brian Webster, thank you for your good ideas, kind heart, and positive attitude.

# Photograph Credits

Cover photograph by Dwayne Congdon; Karsten Heuer: pages 82 and 93; Whyte Museum of the Canadian Rockies: pages 46, 51, 57, 62, and 71.

# About the Author

Helen Rolfe lives with her family in Canmore, Alberta. She too felt the pull of the Rocky Mountains, and moved west from Ontario in her early twenties. She has been there ever since.

# OTHER AMAZING STORIES

These titles are available wherever you buy books. If you have trouble finding the book you want, call the Altitude order desk at 1-800-957-6888, e-mail your request to: orderdesk@altitudepublishing.com or visit our Web site at www.amazingstories.ca

All titles retail for $9.95 Cdn or $7.95 US. (Prices subject to change.)

New AMAZING STORIES titles are published every month. If you would like more information, e-mail your name and mailing address to: amazingstories@altitudepublishing.com.